'I have met hatred, and I chose love.'

JACQUES ROZENBERG

A tribute

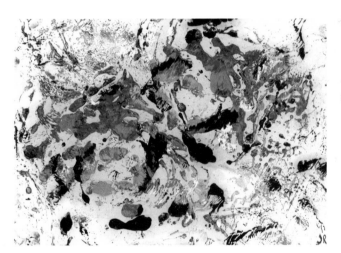

Painting and thought

Conceived and introduced by Andrée Caillet
Translated by Ian Higgins

ONE WHO HAS PASSED THROUGH DEATH, AND IS ALIVE *

Alive in his contradictions, his fury at atrocity, at all war and injustice, his often misunderstood need for affection, his need to communicate – above all with young people.

He was a tormented soul even as a youth, but he adored the music the war stopped him studying, the violin he found it so hard to take up again, the beauty he so admired, and that rarity, true friendship.

After the Death March, Jacques was liberated at Dachau on the eve of 1st May 1945 – propitious day indeed; but his time at Auschwitz had marked him for life.

The memory of those years filled his mind, day and night.

Like many other survivors, he was in demand as a speaker, and for years he went round schools recounting his experiences.
Doing this brought memory to fruition: exhorting youngsters never to forget the events of the past, he urged them to prevent a recurrence of such evil by committing to the love of others.

As he grew older and illness implacably caught up with him, he started writing and painting.
Each painting has a corresponding text; the pictures are small, the texts concentrated. The aim was to deploy a number of themes in a sensuous interplay of colours, predominantly red.

The colour of blood and sudden light.
The contrast between life and death.
All the time, this life–death contrast as sensed there and then.
And all the time, violent splashes – eyes.
Eyes everywhere. His eyes?
Yours, perhaps?
Everywhere, scrutinising the world.

His writing and painting are certainly transpositions of his experience of the hell of the camps, in the nightmarish visions, the tormented lines, the questions, the sudden shouts and cries.
They are his answer to the crucial question: 'How to write and paint after Auschwitz?'

But he also uses subtle variations to celebrate nature – love of life, involvement and commitment, in tonalities which, while bright, are gentle and affectionate.

So he used an imagination fed on memories and dreams to fill countless sheets of paper and even, more originally, his own X-rays.
Gouache or oil, his is an emotive art.

Before he died, he and his wife decided they would endow a Foundation to help young people, regardless of race or creed, embodying the key words he always returned to: 'Love and Generosity'.
They named it **Fondation 'Mains ouvertes – Dignité de vie'** ('Open-Handedness – Dignity of Life').

Another initiative is the 'Jacques Rozenberg Prize', awarded annually, in conjunction with the Belgian Auschwitz Foundation, to the author of a university thesis.

ANDRÉE CAILLET-ROZENBERG
BOARD OF TRUSTEES, BELGIAN NETWORK OF FOUNDATIONS

* quoted from Jorge Semprun

From my violin heart
Have come sounds of suffering
But, as well, of happiness, of loving,
And, now with no trace of shame,
Laughing and crying.

Love can wipe atrocity away,
Saves mankind from powerlessness,
Spurs us on to confront
Ourselves
And others.

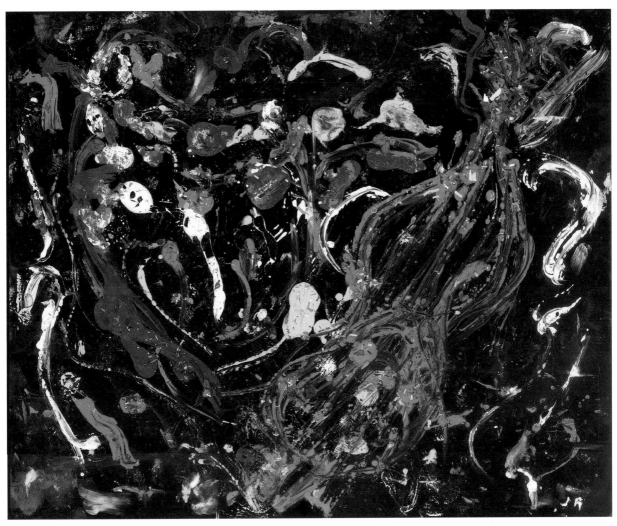

Cello-woman (painted on an X-ray photograph)

Sixty years ago, the Nazi death camps were liberated by the Allies. The world discovered atrocity and horror at their most vile. With the long nightmare of years of war and suffering barely over, the unspeakable image of the very worst that human beings are capable of was flung in our faces.

Jacques Rozenberg had actually experienced that unimaginable, inexplicable hell. And lived. To bear witness, in the name of all the others…

As the 40s dawned, Jacques Rozenberg was one of those young people who, refusing to accept the hijacking of freedom and democracy, resolved to say No to Nazism and occupation.

It was not that they were aspiring heroes.

All they wanted was to live normal lives.

For Jacques Rozenberg, life was music, the violin. Not war!

But circumstances decided otherwise, circumstances dictated his actions.

His determination to resist found concrete expression in the underground press.

But opposition was not without risk. The Nazis exacted a heavy price: two years in an extermination camp, and the Death March.

Resist. We today also have many reasons for 'joining the Resistance'. History, as they say, does endlessly repeat itself.

Certain ills that have afflicted our society tend to creep insidiously back in different guise. Each time, drastic remedies are needed.

The course of History shows how dear it can cost us not to react.

The far right, again and forever, the fault lines in globalisation, inequalities, injustice, self-absorption – so many evils to fight! We have as many reasons to say No as there were in 1940.

Young people especially, tomorrow's adults, have to fight for a fairer society, united in justice.

Every young person has a contribution to make, however grand or humble, towards building a better world!

If we want our young people to exercise this citizenship and secure the future of democracy, we have to encourage them, and support them in whatever role they may play in society.

In this respect, education is certainly a lever. Jacques Rozenberg readily understood this, for many years taking his message into schools.
As Minister of Education, I am very sensitive to the need for us to train pupil citizens, inculcated with respect for the values of democracy.

The present volume will certainly contribute to this. Symbolising a just cause with the example of experiences like Jacques Rozenberg's does prove more effective: people respond more readily if brought directly face to face with an intrinsically inspiring story.
This inspiration will be a wellspring of ideas for the present generation and those to come.

For many young people, the names Auschwitz or Dachau do not fully evoke the reality of what happened.
This is serious. Above all it is worrying, at a time when we are increasingly threatened by all kinds of extremism.
Now, as Jacques Rozenberg's last remaining comrades-in-survival leave us, it is more urgent than ever to fan the flame of memory and revive our vigilance!

PRESIDENT OF THE FRANCOPHONE COMMUNITY OF BELGIUM

MINISTER FOR PENSIONS, CITIES AND SOCIAL INTEGRATION
OF THE FEDERAL GOVERNMENT SINCE MARCH 2008

MARIE ARENA

As the 20th century drew to a close, two peoples were exterminated,
one in eastern Europe, the other in eastern Africa,
A white people by whites, a black people by blacks.
And twice, the world remained indifferent.
Connivance, genocide.

Jacques Rozenberg survived extreme evil, in rage and in hope.
Counting on the power of words, sounds and colours.
He cries out in revolt and speaks of faith, paints joy and sings of love.

It is an honour to be asked to write a preface for his work and to bring
together, through that work, the Jewish and Rwandan peoples.

Witness, resistance, love of life and, perhaps, prevention of a
recurrence.

Brussels, 13 January 2005

Emmanuel KAYITANA IMANZI
Ambassador of the Republic of Rwanda
to Benelux, the European Union and the Holy See.

Don't cry – you'll get out,
one way or another!

From the chairman of the belgian auschwitz foundation

Who was Jacques Rozenberg?

I can justly claim to have known him well. Our families were very close, both active in Bundist circles. That was how we learned the rudiments of Yiddish, the Jewish vernacular of eastern Europe. Jacques' parents separated, and he suffered from the ensuing uprootedness. He lived with his mother in a small flat over a baker's shop. He and his friend Henri, the landlord's son, were talented violinists, always competing to see who could play the better.

Already his own man, Jacques decided he would come along with me to the Faucons rouges (affiliated to the International Falcon Movement). We went on summer camps together. But he was never one for taking orders, and when he wanted a bit of freedom he would just go off for a while.

We lost touch during the war.

Once back in Nazi-occupied Belgium, I enrolled at the Free University of Brussels. There I was given the task of organising a resistance move-ment. Jacques got involved via the underground press. I learned later that, like me, he had been caught. Miraculously, we both returned from captivity, and he married an Italian girl. We resumed close ties with the setting up of an association of concentration-camp survivors from Auschwitz and Upper Silesia. This was when I learned that it was being a gifted violinist that had spared him selection in the camps. These same musical gifts were to make him the obvious person to direct the regional record library in Brussels. He did not let the growing threat of illness stop him doing volunteer work for Oxfam, or setting up, with comrades from the Association of Survivors, the Auschwitz Foundation, of which I am honoured to be Chairman. This was no small undertaking; sadly, most of those involved have now passed away.

After his divorce, he found support in Andrée. She helped him discover his talents for writing and poetry as well as painting. So it was that he came to use a special technique of painting on X-ray photographs, as well as on paper.

There is little more to tell. His suffering worsened right to the end, but he continued to bear witness, that there might never be another Auschwitz.

Jacques, we miss you. Critical minds are rare, enriching, and indispensable.

Baron Paul Halter

To the memory of Jacques Rozenberg and all the Victims of Fascism

Throughout history, some men have borne a burden out of all proportion to what others have had to shoulder. Some of those men were proclaimed heroes, but most lived more modest lives, away from the gaze of a too often forgetful public.

The burdens and sufferings of those men have brought freedom and hope to those of us who lived normal, uneventful lives. We must never forget the gratitude we owe them for their strength and courage.

Jacques Rozenberg was one of those men, enduring more than flesh and blood can stand – and yet he survived. He overcame his sufferings in Auschwitz and Dachau, and through his paintings and poems he succeeded in giving artistic expression to his emotions. For this too, for sharing his thoughts and sorrows through his works, we owe him thanks.

Although Jacques Rozenberg readily gave many interviews, and considered it his bounden duty to meet students in schools and tell them about his experiences, he was not one to hold forth in company about his years in the extermination camps. But you still sensed that his soul was full of pain and sorrow from what he had experienced.

Thanks to his wife Andrée Caillet, this book is now a reality in English. I hope that the reader will take a few moments to reflect on Jacques Rozenberg and those men who bore their burdens in loneliness so that we can continue our lives in hope and freedom.

All honour to the memory of Jacques Rozenberg!

Hanne JENSBO
President Elect of Soroptimist International

Jacques Rozenberg

'The time has come
When I to sulphurous and tormenting flames
Must render up myself.'*

The medieval idea of Hell is hard to visualise. In the folk memory it appears like a gigantic fiery furnace, guarded by black demons with pitch-forks, a place from which there is no escape.

The victims were cast down there for having sinned, or for turning away from the face of God.

The twentieth century overturned this notion.

Hell was found to be not somewhere else, like the hereafter (always supposing that that exists) but in the very world we live in, for some in their own streets, as one part of humanity turned against another part.

There were no supernatural demons, only other living human beings, made inhumane by demonic ideologies; no pitchforks, but machine guns and rifles; everyday lorries and trains were mobilised to transport the 'damned'.

There was no punishment for lives ill-lived – some of the wisest and most beautiful people were arrested – their only 'crime' being born into a race which did not suit other races. So the language was perverted, and words like 'solution' and 'cleansing' came to mean something else.

No work of art can ever convey the horror of the Holocaust.

After the war there were the photographs – the empty rail tracks, the deserted camps, the piles of boots, the emanciated survivors... and the statistics.

But what was it like to suffer this nightmare?

We can only rely on the witnesses.

14

My father was in the trenches in the first world war. He wouldn't speak about it. He gave me a book of Wilfred Owen's poetry. 'It's all in there,' he said.

Nowadays I live two streets away from Anne Frank's house. I knew an old actress who remembered her as a little girl. Nowadays hundreds of people visit her 'hide-out' every day – they've read her diaries, telling us what daily life in occupied Amsterdam was like, as seen from the inside. And here is Jacques Rozenberg. He saw Auschwitz from the inside. He wrote about it. He painted it. He was a witness. He brings it closer to us than any amount of statistics.

"It must never happen again," we say. But although the great conflagration of the Holocaust is over, there are still many fires blazing all over the world. Genocides, massacres, gassings – where inhuman men are still sending their fellows to hell, because of their race.

ADRIAN BRINE
PLAY DIRECTOR
ENGLAND
BELGIUM – NETHERLANDS

* 'Hamlet' (The Ghost.)

'Perasma'. Pierre Mertens. © Éditions du Seuil – 2001
From pp. 542–544.
The character Tobias is modelled on Jacques, whom the author knew so
well.

Summer had just returned for a moment, when the telephone knifed into
it. I thought afterwards that I shouldn't have answered. It was Richard.
He said straight out he was sorry to be ringing with 'bad news'. Tobias
had died, after his last study trip to Auschwitz. My mind instantly filled
with all my memories of him, all those lasting ties between us. So, I
thought, he had just died, with the millennium almost upon us, when
over half a century earlier he had been the best part of three years in
Auschwitz and on the 'Death March', and survived. Yes: which was the
more surprising – that he hadn't died then, or that he had now?

I'd only ever known him as someone still alive. A miraculous survivor. I'd
hardly met him – I was looking for the score of Janáček's 'Intimate
Letters' quartet and went into his music shop – before learning he was
a survivor. From Auschwitz. (As if he'd been born and bred there, and
only recently left.) Neither of us ever knew what made us confide in one
another ('confess' would be a better word).
Yet it was our shared love of music that had got us talking. 'Ah, you like
Janáček, do you? And Bartók's last quartets as well. Are you a musician,
then?'
I had a list of records scribbled on a piece of paper, and he must have
read it upside down. There was even Messiaen's Mode de valeurs et
d'intensités! 'You'll have to wait for that, there's not much demand for
it.'
'I'm not a musician, but I can read music.'
'One way of playing an instrument – any instrument, in fact! Don't you
think so?'
No, I didn't. And here is why: Once, not so long ago, Tobias *had* played
the violin. And that was what had saved his life in the camp, because
he'd been able to play tunes the butchers liked. 'But I haven't played
since getting back, of course...'. Of course he hadn't. It was so obvious.

He couldn't any longer let his violin be heard in or for a world that had perpetrated what it had. So the last people to have had the privilege of hearing the musician Tobias Goldberg were actually his tormentors.

'Why don't you learn an instrument? You're still young... And it's very satisfying in all sorts of ways.'
'But – what about you?'
'Oh, it's different for me. Your situation's not the same as mine, is it? I can't make my fingers do what I want now. These days, I paint.'
'And you can make...'
'They can manage that, yes.'

Our paths rarely crossed. There's no need for frequent meetings with someone whose sole concern is with what is utterly essential. The essence of evil, the essence of good. Auschwitz and music. Music at Auschwitz. Auschwitz in music. Music in spite of Auschwitz.
His life was punctuated by courses of medical treatment and pilgrimages with groups of teenagers to the death camps, where he showed them round like a museum guide. Revealed horror and atrocity to them, in a dead, slightly monotonous voice. Somebody had to do it: after him and his comrades, who else would take it on? It would be as if nothing had ever happened. It wasn't just another 'page in a history book', was it? Which could be handed from one generation to the next... 'So even the Holocaust came to an end' (he added, with a peculiar grating laugh; a good joke from the depths of hell).
One day, choosing my words very carefully, I made so bold as to ask him if he wasn't afraid that, with his precarious health, all these 'excursions', these regular journeys back to the capital of absolute Infamy, would eventually wear him out. His answer was that what would really destroy his health would be to miss these engagements – that was what would make him feel he was done for. I got the impression that he was no longer choosing between what was good or bad for him, but determining where the lesser evil lay... Visiting his dead: yes, it was a dreadful ordeal, every time. But forgetting them, even just once by chance, or one year in two – that was unthinkable.

PIERRE

Jacques, my Friend,

Do you remember the spring of 1992? Do you remember our visit to Auschwitz? I was with six young North Africans, three boys and three girls. It was the first time young Moroccans had been on a study trip with the Auschwitz Foundation. You were one of twelve concentration camp survivors.

While some were afraid of how these young North Africans might react, you weren't. Because you knew how to listen, and how to recount the most horrible things very simply.

Jacques! When I have forgotten everything else, our meeting and that journey will remain imprinted in the very core of my memory. And you have dared to ask me why?

I'll give just three reasons.
First, throughout the whole of that trip, you never once spoke a wounding or scornful word when you talked about your tormentors. You taught me never to hate.

The second reason is the hope you placed in mankind: you were a universalist who must surely have done a lot of thinking. You know, Jacques, every time I quote Albert Einstein's 'It is easier to split the atom than to break a prejudice', I think of you doing all that thinking about who you were.

And finally: we were standing where two paths crossed. Our guide was describing the route the prisoners took to the gas chambers; he stopped speaking for a moment and then continued: 'Right here, where we are standing, is where they walked to their deaths', and every one of us backed away. And at that moment a tear trickled down Zohra's cheek. You were standing next to her, and you reached out and gently, affectionately, lifted the tear off with your fingertip.

Oh, Jacques! If we were all like you, I'm sure war would be banished from this earth. You knew that the obstacles to peace are in the hearts and minds of human beings.

MAHFOUD ROMDHANI
VICE-PRESIDENT OF THE FRANCOPHONE PARLIAMENT
OF THE REGION OF BRUSSELS CAPITAL

MAKING MUCH FROM VERY LITTLE
A TRANSLATOR'S VIEW

Theodor Adorno's assertion that 'after Auschwitz, to write a poem is barbaric' contains two implicit questions: is it not to show disrespect to the millions of victims to write, say, about the beauty of Nature instead of giving them voice? and how can language, bankrupt from use and abuse, express the inexpressible evil that 1945 has revealed to us? As it turns out, many writers, including poets, have found honourable answers to these questions. Indeed, expressing the seemingly inexpressible, whether good or evil, has arguably always been the ultimate aim of poetry. At all events, the paintings and texts published here are, as Andrée Caillet says, Jacques Rozenberg's own answer to the crucial question: 'How to write and paint after Auschwitz?' Which of course confronts his translator with an equally crucial question: how to convey the 'hows' of Rozenberg's texts?

One striking feature of the textual material is its generic variety. Brief pieces of narrative, generally in prose but sometimes in verse, intermingle with evocations of life in the camp, aphoristic reflections on the private and public implications of Rozenberg's experience, celebrations of – yes – the beauty of Nature, music and love, and exhortations to respect the victims' memory by never giving up the struggle against intolerance. Many of these texts are in verse, or so broken up as to read like verse. Are they poems? Some undoubtedly are; many more, if not poems, have poetic qualities. However one labels them, they all share a certain tone – neither strident nor declamatory, but quiet, restrained, sometimes disconcertingly matter-of-fact, as in this example: 'Only a few of the children are trapped for captivity. / They will be guinea-pigs, / Till pushed in their turn into the death chamber.' The expressivity of such texts springs from the contrast between this tone and what we already know, and is not said, about the things the text refers to – here, the fact that most of the children were sent straight to the gas chambers on arrival.

The variation in genre, and Rozenberg's use of understatement and implication, build up an impression of fragmentariness. The texts are like shards of life. But there are phrases and themes that recur, so that gradually the shards reassemble into a fragile, constantly threatened but tough-minded coherence.

One function of the fragmentariness – both between texts and, often, within them – is to embody the limited resources offered by language. So the combative vulnerability into which the fragments cohere does in itself turn those very limitations to account. And similar observations apply, mutatis mutandis, both to the paintings which accompany the texts and to the relation between painting and text – each, in effect, is context to the other. But where Rozenberg really takes language by the scruff of the neck is in the various forms of word-play which characterise many of the texts – rhyme, assonance, multiple meanings and, above all, puns. Here is an example, taken from a short text on p. 129:

> D'autres se sont dit: vaudrait mieux mourir.
> Enfin. En fin. En faim.

In its context, the first line is straightforward enough: 'Some reckoned: better off dead.' But not the second. A literal translation might be: 'At last. At the end. In hunger.' But this misses much of the point, because the three French expressions are phonically identical – three sounds, in the same order, spoken three times, but with three different meanings. The puns, and the grating humour they generate, are essential to the overall meaning, and cannot be conveyed with a literal translation; only some form of inventive compensation, corresponding to Rozenberg's own creativeness, might do:

> Starving... Starving... Starved.
> Dead.

This is by no means the most complex example of Jacques Rozenberg's word-play, nor is it the richest in thematic implications or emotional resonance. But it is an appropriate illustration of the function of his punning technique. For there is a close analogy in such cases between style and subject matter. Not surprisingly, a major theme in the book is need, scarcity, want, starvation. Not enough clothes, food, medicine or shelter; and no freedom, not even to sing or to hum (see p. 119). The recourse to pun and other word-play exemplifies the imperative to make much out of very little. Pun is a particularly suitable way of giving language this symbolic function because language is in some respects so limited: there is a finite stock of words and grammatical structures at our disposal, but, in principle, an infinity of experience to express. Might it even be the case that, as some theorists have argued, it is language itself, not the speaker or writer, that produces the utterance? Word play, especially punning, suggests not. Pun is perhaps the supreme manifestation of subjectivity, an individual's creative agency, in language. Making much from very little: like the textual fragmentariness, Rozenberg's punning is a way of denying scarcity by transforming it, by exploiting it to affirm the resilience, the individuality, that the system in the camps had been intended to destroy. While Rozenberg talks in many of his texts about his struggle, and the need to continue it, the texts themselves actually embody it.

As with the texts, so with many of the paintings. As emblematic an example as 'Enfin. En fin. En faim' is the painting entitled 'To live in disguise!' (p. 79). Like pun, disguise is a mode of transformation. The need for disguise and dissimulation is a motif in the book. It is obviously relevant to captivity; less obviously, and all the more distressingly, it is just as relevant to trying to live a life after Auschwitz. The motif is embodied in the quasi-surrealist fluidity and ambiguity of this painting. In the top third of the image, slightly left of centre, there is a kind of face. Keep looking at it, and it dissolves and re-forms into at least five different faces which emerge, disappear and re-emerge endlessly – and this quite apart from the other faces, masks and eyes floating elsewhere in the picture.

How to write after Auschwitz? Rozenberg's answer to this question was to ask, text by text, two others: 'How did I survive?' and 'Why?' The second question in particular is unanswerable; Rozenberg would surely have said, with Primo Levi, that 'if for no other reason than that an Auschwitz existed, no one in our age should speak of providence'. Be that as it may, how he asks the questions is everything. It is the translator's task to convey that 'how' – the making of much from very little, the linguistic resourcefulness and all it conveys: courage; generosity of spirit; the temptation to self-pity; humour; love of beauty; the determination to keep on fighting for a more humane world. It is an honour to have been entrusted with this exacting and inspiring responsibility.

Ian HIGGINS
University of St Andrews (United Kingdom)

Humanity is just as fragile as strong
Some people are brave, others craven torturers
All, let us all be vigilant, lest humanity be pushed into inhumanity.

Seeing death so close, so often, has strengthened my passionate wish
to live and pass on the lessons of my time in the camps.
A passion, a struggle for a more humane society, which I am glad to
share with you.

Seeing is not knowing
knowing is not thinking
thinking is not acting
Let us act together for life, the birthright of all, with love and humour
and all its joys to defend it.

As protagonist of a personal and collective memory, it is not enough for
me to preserve it, my duty is to tell it, lest the future be repetition of
past horrors and deaths.
And yet already...

L'homme est tant fragile
que fort
Les uns étant courageux
D'autres de lâches bourreaux
Soyez, soyons vigilants
afin d'éviter de le placer
en situation inhumaine

Je me suis si souvent
trouvé proche de la mort
que celle ic conforter m'aragie
de vivre et de transmettre
les leçons tirées de mon parcours
concentrationnaire
Cette rage, cette lutte pour
une société plus humaine
Je les partage volontiers avec
vous

Voir n'est pas savoir
savoir n'est pas réfléchir
réfléchir n'est pas agir
Agissons ensemble
pour la vie, droit pour
tous avec
Ses joies, l'amour et
l'humour pour défense

Acteur d'une mémoire
personnelle et collective
la conserver ne peut suffire,
la dire est un devoir
afin d'éviter que l'avenir
ne devienne la répétition
d'un passé d'horreur et de morts.
Et pourtant déjà...

Magnolia Clinic, Brussels, July 1999

23

April 1945.
After two years, habituated at length
to daily horror and humiliation,
to total, utter degradation.

A face shattered and crushed – my face,
slashed with wounds and scars,
some visible, some invisible.
The eyes, bathed in blood
outside and in,
ooze a look of impotent rage.

April 1998.
Photo taken on one of my returns to Auschwitz.
A study trip with a mixed group of French- and Dutch-speaking
teachers.

If I hadn't dreamed dreams – yes, even there.
If I hadn't made up those crazy stories
and let the insanest fantasies run free.
If chance hadn't been there for me.
If…
I wouldn't be here, with you.

Shattered face

Auschwitz
Execution yard

PART ONE

Auschwitz, absolute negation

I have to talk,
I have to talk about it.
Today,
Tomorrow,
For people to know
And remember
That the worst can happen again.

Auschwitz.

Arrive at first light.
Out barely conscious from the sealed waggons
They had packed us into,
Still human beings, for shipment.
Dogs raging. SS men baying.

Selection.
The great question mark.

You, left; you, right.
Right side, wrong side,
Heads, tails.

On the ramp, a family, knowing only fear
As their fates are toyed with.
Huddled in a tight, tight clasp.
Being together.
Keep together.

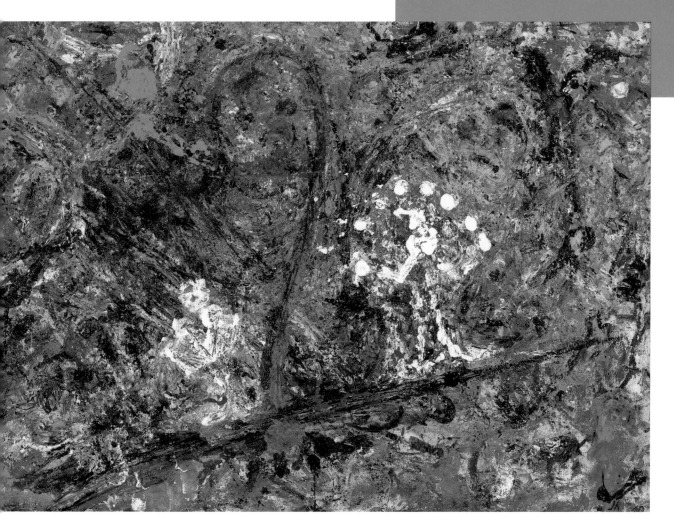

Women, children, the elderly,

All the unproductive for German firms.

From this very day

All they leave will be footprints on the ground.

Only a few of the children are trapped for captivity.

They will be guinea-pigs,

Till pushed in their turn into the death chamber.

Gassed, asphyxiated, burnt –

If not already murdered, in medical experiments.

Respect.

Silence.

Let their cries be heard at last.

A new day much like all the others dawns,

Following a night of anxieties and doubts, not rest –

And shadows shuffle forward

Like the slaves they are, condemned

To all the tortures:

Beatings, hunger, cold.

Despair.

Dragging feet,

Backs bent, reduced to zombies.

Wrong side, right side.

Accidents expected to be frequent.

Death continuous.

The kapo shouts, deals out beatings.

He's not dog-tired…

Besides, he thinks it'll save his skin.

Wrong side, right side.

Fit for cut-price slavery.

A man has come through the questioning.

To survive,

He needs rapidly to work out rules

For how a concentration camp works.

Some less exhausting labour,

Some spat-out scrap to eat,

An SS guard's reject,

Mouldy, uneatable.

Shame endured in soundless tears.

What has life at twenty proved to be?

Barely lived.

Kitted out in stripes.

Tattooed with a number.

Here I am. Staring numbly at incomprehensibility.

The hundred-flood blood of hell, thousand-flood, unending flood.

How did I take all that and not give in?

All my life, that's the question I've never stopped asking.

Why?

Your whole being is here. Here or... somewhere else!

Survive the present moment with no certainty
of a next one.
I could not accept dying there, in Auschwitz.
'The sheer injustice,' I kept telling myself.

Only one life, it was there to be lived.
Even if it stopped where the camp did.

Blazing camp

With the imminent arrival of American troops from the north and the
Soviets from the east,

a camp is set on fire, block by block, by the SS,

who want to leave no trace of life behind them,

no trace of industrialised death –

when the ground is red with fire and gorged with blood.

On one of our halts on the Death March,

I see in the distance barbed wire that has withstood this destructive
fury,

and the arms of carbonised trees stretching up towards

an incandescent sky.

MY FIRST DAY ON THE DEATH MARCH FROM JAWORZNO TO DACHAU

The worst of the worst, the Death March – or rather, the Death Marches. For there were differences even here, just as there were in the camps, where 1942 wasn't 1943 (the worst two years), and 1944 wasn't as hard as 1943. For some, it lasted a month, for others almost three. But for all, it was full of indescribable suffering.

Mid-January 1945.
In the evening, artillery fire; the Soviets are getting close.
We are assembled into a column. Surrounded by SS guards, we leave the satellite camp of Jaworzno, me with a whole loaf pushed down inside my shirt next to my skin, and a blanket over my shoulders. Had someone given me the blanket, or did I steal it? The people from the sick bay, at the rear of the column, can barely stand.

I'm not a historian. I'm simply telling you what my memory has preserved from the first twenty-four hours.

The column sets off along the road. Clogs scrape the snow. It's minus 20 or 25 or 30. The start of an incredible forced march, punctuated with executions as the SS shoot anyone who can't go any further, and even those who are too weak to keep up the pace. No more privileges here: the horror is just as great for those who'd been in charge of barracks, dormitories or labour gangs. Justice at last???
At dawn, the guards stop us outside a barn. The doors are opened. There's a stampede to get into shelter.
Packed in, squashed against one another or on top of one another, the prisoners whimper and pee. Nobody speaks. But not everyone could get in, including me.
Nothing for it but to lie down in the snow, wrapped in the blanket. And still this visceral anger, this raging will to live, to survive injustice, that has never once deserted me through all my time in the camps and will, yet again, get me through the next few hours and back onto my feet. Still this good luck?

Then the barn doors are pulled open and my comrades come back out, apart from those who've been crushed under the weight of the others, or else been strangled by someone who wanted the bread they hadn't the strength to do more than nibble at.

And the march resumes, as far as the next village, where the mayor gives out two frostbitten beets per person, a sure guarantee of diarrhoea.

Once more the march resumes.

We're in a trance, almost insane. Dragging themselves along like ghosts, some have linked arms.

My neighbour on the left turns to me and says: 'Look, they're not the SS, they're Red Army soldiers leading us to freedom!'

Then the one on my right says: 'If only we could go back to our own camp at Jaworzno!'

Night has fallen. I'll say no more of those first twenty-four hours. It would take days to tell the story of the next two and a half months of torture, and the four camps where by rights I should have died a hundred times before I was liberated on 30 April, at Dachau. Like a boxer saved by the bell who staggers back to his corner to get the bleeding stopped, determined to fight on, I was determined yet again to beat death.

If the talk is to be of solidarity and human dignity, you won't find them in the concentration or extermination camps, except for a few rare individuals or groups.

Here, with you today and tomorrow, is where that dignity and that solidarity must manifest themselves, in reaction against the obscene monsters of Nazism, fascism and all authoritarianism. They have long been on the prowl, and will prowl for a long time yet unless we fight them. Auschwitz-Birkenau – the biggest cemetery in the world, it's been said. 'Cemetery' means silence, peace, company.

No, Auschwitz-Birkenau is an empty place, sodden with blood and covered with the ashes of millions screaming 'Not this, not ever again'. Listen to them.

That's all we wanted.

Alas!

Dachau, March 1933 – The first camp to be opened.
Dachau, April 1945 – One of the last to be liberated.

30 April. The first day of my deliverance.
The sky clears. At last.

The Americans enter the camp and liberate over thirty thousand
exhausted or dying prisoners, of twenty-seven different
nationalities, including many political prisoners.

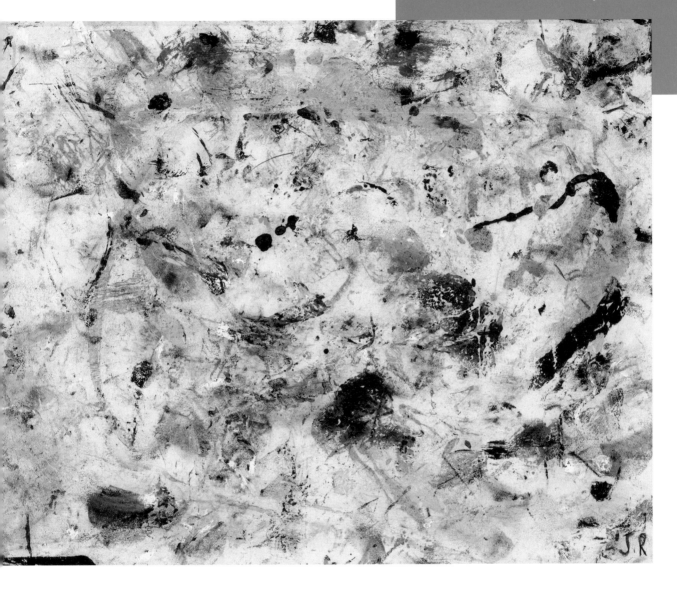

The captive and the robot guarding him

In this incoherent world,

We are given one chance to get through it all... and everything else!

So one person's survival is sometimes at the expense of another's.

Pain. Revolt. Hope. Life after the event...

Having been entrained for death, how to retrain for life?

A whole past life to surmount, to conquer!

Act as if.

Act as if you're the same as everyone else.

The ones who didn't go through it.

Trains now were just for taking our problems from place to place.

Back in the world of civilisation,

Or civil lies and violation,

We were the flotsam of dreams of brotherhood and peace,

But few took any interest in us,

In our state of mind, or even body.

We were left to our own devices.

No reception centres,

No squads of doctors or psychologists

To listen and help.

Trains now were just for getting away, no matter where.

Headlong away

To escape

The useless toings and froings

And then back again.

The main thing is, I'm alive… and you believe it.
Heart to heart with love, I've eased gently back.

You've read me aright.
Lifewards-leading voices
Reading lifewards-leading maps.

50 years on, round the camp, life has triumphed over death.

Can we believe it?

Eventually I've had to,

Except when I've felt myself dissolving...

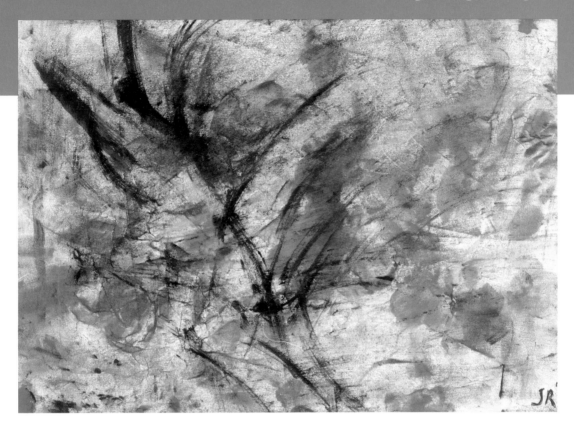

Season by season,

Year after year,

Nature has grown green again.

Everything grows.

Everything grows back.

Reality.

How good, to breathe for one more day, then perhaps another,
and another...

To breathe to paint, and write, escape the nauseating present.

Thus have I repainted and written down my life,
Written and repainted Life sometimes
In colours and settings dreamed up by me.

Hope!

57

To be heard,

Heard and understood.

Finding myself so often face to face with organised death

Has strengthened my wish to pass on the lessons learned.

My raging will to live.

A manifold anger, suppressed, explosive,

Distressed, aggressive,

Seductive, destructive.

My incessant anger.

My endless battling, for greater justice.

Keep quiet by night.
So easy.

Keep it quiet by day.
So cowardly.

All sorts to make a world.
Vile world.

The writhing swarm of the vile.

Yesterday, today. Tomorrow?

Abetting the authoritarian,

The totalitarian.

Here, there,

Bathed in all the colours of daylight.

Present everywhere, a menace

Which the complacent, the weak, the naïve, the timid

Do not see.

The writing swarm of the vile.

Bodies tangled, violated, in a vortex of pain and injustice.

Today is like yesterday: a shambles.

You're playing 'pretend I don't know'.
Or even blocking off your heart and mind:
Life, a life for you and yours, is enough.

The blood is flowing that has never ceased to flow.

What have we understood? What have we learnt?

What do you mean, 'Never again'?
You're having a laugh!

That phrase, parroted,
Over and over,
Has lost all meaning as brother fights brother,
From war to rebellion and back.
The populations starving, oppressed, destroyed.

When can we ever stop fighting *against*,
And start fighting *for*?

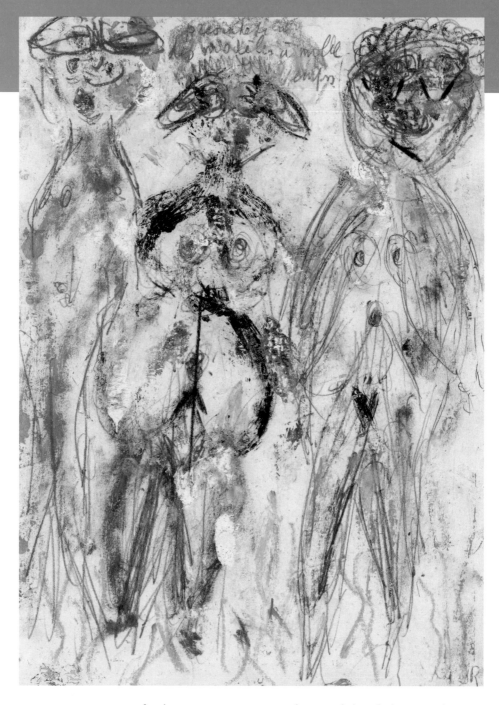

And now, we present: the models of the very latest
Multi-phase, multi-facet, fashion.
Is the emphasis more on the seen than the hidden?
Or vice-versa?

Multiple faces

Multiple faces may appear singular.

The singular settling for the plural.

My sad clowns, giving laughter, give in to it

And to death.

Isn't that the limit, to suffer

From laughing!

Nothing for it but to cry.

Le carnaval défoule :
mes clowns sont tristes
à en rire

Appearances flaunted,

Pot-belly sported,

Clothes hung on doors,

Gates swung in forts –

Comparisons borne, disguises worn

Never last.

Fullness from void:

Endless toil.

Fruitless,

Void!

The Loch Ness monster does not exist.

It's just another image spawned by human fear.

And yet it has been seen,

Blind people say.

How good to live in disguise!

A well-ordered life, and unobserved.

In all conscience well deserved.

Which a little charity will justify.

There must be no seeing.

No knowing.

No understanding.

No hearing…

The silence.

The terrible silence

Of man's

Indifference

To man.

The innocent hide behind masks.

Human monsters do exist,

Proliferate.

And yet

They are unseen.

Unsuspected even.

Nobody wants to know.

If the world's turned unbearable,

Turn the page!

Battle to live

Lovingly and with warmth.

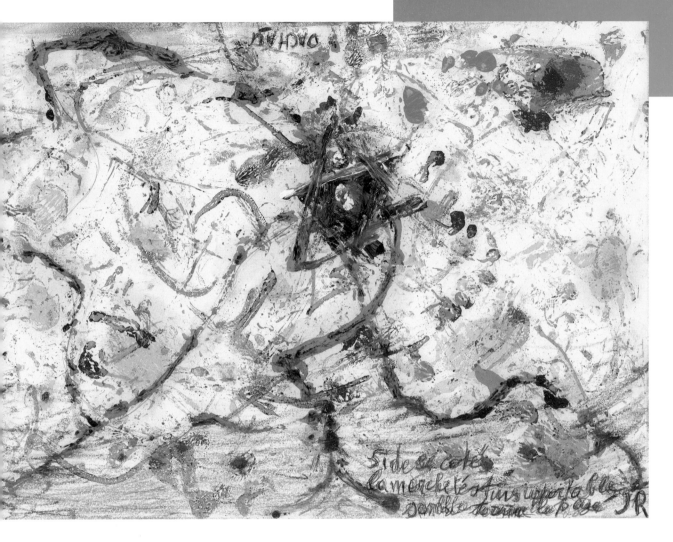

Mustn't rebel against injustice, whatever happens.

And yet you – yes you, looking at this picture – you have two hands.

Open the left one wide and hold it out

To those who, like you,

Are working for a world of brotherhood.

Clench your right fist,

Clench it hard,

There's a fight to be fought

Against others' refusal.

The dream of Don Quixote

Don Quixote on his horse,

A butt to all contrariety,

Rebelled against it.

When others stay submerged,

He fights, head high, looking skywards

In quest of the absolute.

The laughing-stock becomes symbol.

Utopian!

Who knows!

Don Quixote opens wide his eyes, alert.
Lance outthrust to run injustice through.

Imagination not totally blind.
Courage not totally vain.

Followed, just about, by Sancho:
Valleys and hills,
Castles and mills.

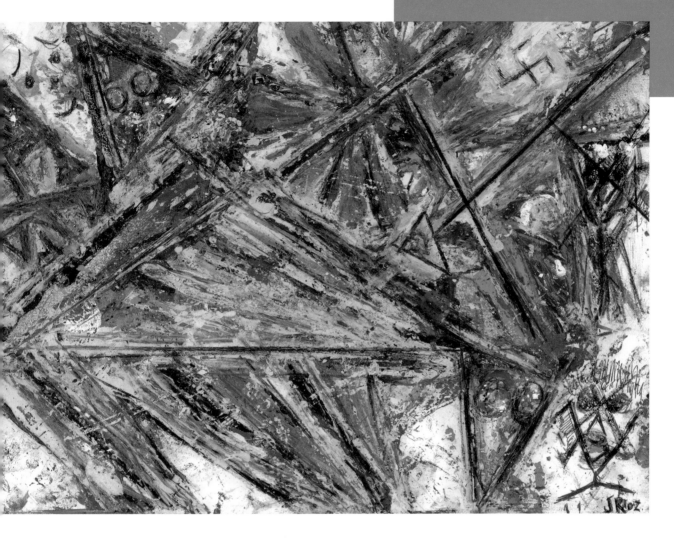

Quixote and Dulcinea

Meet.

Looks exchanged.

Words spoken.

Understood.

Helped or hindered by his Flame,

Shall he gain the impossible dream?

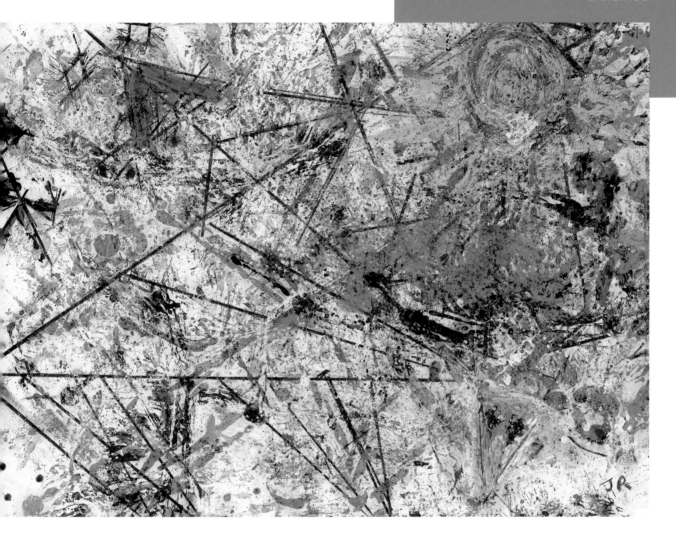

It's not enough to be somewhere else.

You still have to find the somewhere.

I'm ill now, shut in, with no emergency exit.

I cough.

My cough explodes, shatters my body,

My heart.

Why? Why me? Well, and why not?

The wind and rain are so stifling

I've lost the use of my limbs.

In the night I'm so frightened I twist and turn this way and that

To try and get my breath back.

I try and sleep for a while

Despite the cramps.

A night for tranquillisers.

A night for plumbing bottomless voids.

Or falling on the floor.

From the depths of my memory horrors come back

That turn my stomach.

From my lips, a cry escapes

I kept muffled for the sake of others.

Get up, so soon…

The day will be so long…

And so short as well.

Tomorrow's knocking at the door already.

The things going on in my head,

You've no idea.

Some days worse than others,

You're clamped by anxiety,

The paralysing fear of being on your own.

When the wind-blown windmill turns,

The flowers thrill, everything turns to song.

Just one note, pleasure is back,

And song sings its way round my mind again.

An A, that sweetest of notes,

Itself a song of happiness,

Enchants my heart,

Enchants my life,

Calms my pain.

My heart begins to sing

Music as celebration.
The song of all the instruments
Given us by nature.

Music in imagination.
One string is enough
To create in my mind
That chord, that harmony
I thrill with.

Music, old helpmeet,
Ever young.
From known to new-found.
All the memories it preserves,
Awakens,
Recovers.

Like Don Quixote on a blazing afternoon,

My little faun wakes up wondering.

Questing for other places,

Wondrous other places.

Sailing over oceans, like me,

He runs before the wind towards a better world

To look for flowers of tenderness,

Delicately brushed

By gentle breezes

Recalling none but dreams of love from the past.

Gentle breeze

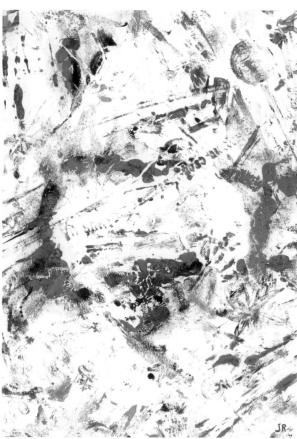

My last wink back at youth
For the joy of being alive, and for generosity.

I looked at the sun,
I saw the rainbow.
My sun makes the flowers grow,
Gives them colour and scentedness.
My rainbow banishes malice, mediocrity and ugliness.
It is the being and gift of happiness.

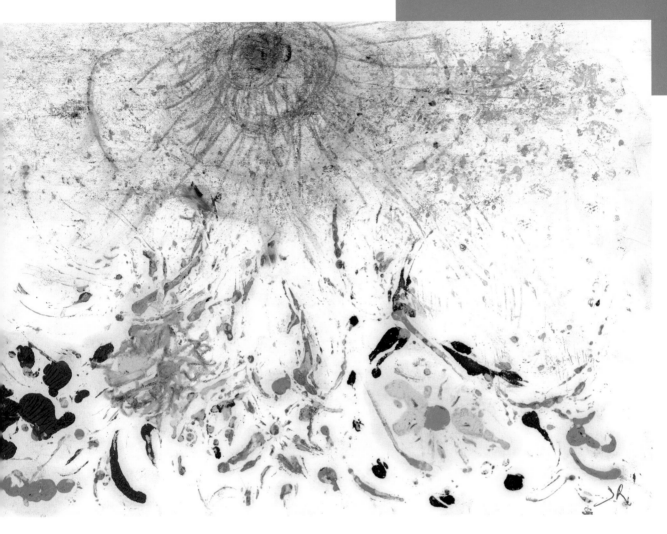

Brussels, August 1999.

Beyond the power of darkness,

Carried off by his ideal,

The little sky-blue man

Is making for infinity.

Humanity is just as fragile as valiant.

Some so courageous.

Others, cowards and torturers.

Never forget. Be ceaselessly vigilant.

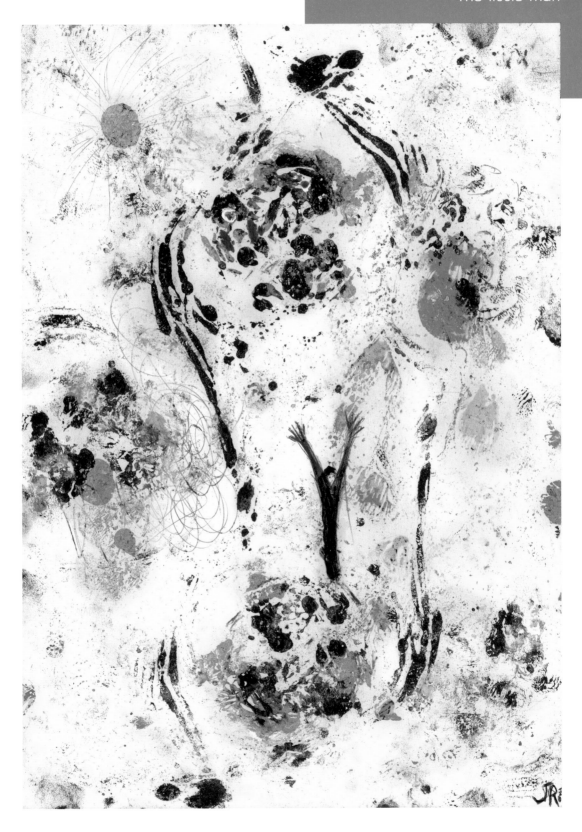

Narratives

On the duty to live and bear witness: Jaworzno

To bear witness

Is to plant one's own grain of experience from the camps
In a furrow traced for a more humane world.

As protagonist of a personal and collective memory,
It is not enough for me to preserve it.

It is a duty to tell it.

Lest the future
Be repetition of past horrors and deaths.

AUSCHWITZ — BLOOD GONE WITH THE HOT AIR

AUSCHWITZ, L'EN PORTE LE VENT

In respectful memory of the eleven builders
hanged at Jaworzno-Auschwitz
on 14 August 1944
for attempting escape.

What is left of memory,
Blurring aleady, scored out,
Way made for nightmare.
What was once the extreme of horror
Looks humdrum now
Beside the horrors we're bludgeoned with today.
Bludgeoned by atrocity, unexplainedly.
Manipulated yet again, by courtesy
Of our quotable varsity lords of the universe.

Man, the all-too-often consummate fool.
Cultured high-flyer and ordinary guy alike.
One, puffed up with learning and know-how,
And so very sure of his power
To shake the world up for the better.
While the ordinary guy gapes hypnotised
At the TV picture
That cannot lie,
The cut-and-paste trickery he's blind to.
All the shifting images that leave him undefended, unwondering, undoubt-
ing.
That's where he finds the truth, his truth.
And sometimes, just a fiver nets him his place in paradise.

How hard it is to have both heart and mind.

Auschwitz — burnt blood, incense still in the wind

Auschwitz, l'en sang présent

There are eleven men in the squad of Polish builders at Jaworzno, a satellite labour camp of Auschwitz.

Ten men and their kapo, all from Katowice or neighbouring villages, interned as socialists and resisters.
Combatants. Antisemites.

Eleven Poles, resisters, socialists, nationalists, and unbelievably anti-semitic.
Eleven privileged men, with a corner to themselves in one of the wooden huts built for the prisoners. My hut.

Enjoying better rations than the other prisoners, the builders were also permitted by the SS to receive food parcels from their families nearby: bread, margarine, sausage. While this arrangement lasted, I was allowed to beg from these men on parcel days, though the parcels were already half-empty when they arrived.

Eleven privileged men, better fed, stronger, whose job was to put up the masonry buildings in the camp.

Jaworzno was a sandy ravine near a power station under construction. The project was run by German bosses and the work supervised by the kapos, themselves under supervision from constant SS patrols.

Also nearby were coal mines which had been flooded for years. Some of us were selected to get the mines operating again, extremely dangerous work. The timbers were rotten, and we were up to our waists in water; if a roof fall didn't kill us, we would die of pneumonia. But that didn't matter — other slaves would take our places straight away.

From the day they arrived, the only Jew tolerated by the builders was me, the little violinist who played waltzes and tangos with the kapo builder — an accordionist — and Janos the guitarist, another builder. Three evenings a week, we played while those who ran the camp danced with young errand-boys — their 'dates'.

This was after a crippling twelve hours of forced labour. Two more hours of exhaustion; all for an extra bowl of water with a potato floating in it, a turnip or two, sometimes a crust left in the bottom of the pot. Sometimes we had the good fortune to play for the SS cook. What a blowout! Thicker soup.

Once rescued from anonymity, I was given a privilege of my own: these eleven builders got me taken on as their labourer.
My job was to throw them bricks for them to stack up. So highly skilled was I that I was struck on the head one day by a brick that one of the men failed to catch.
An episode that has clearly left its mark.

But my main job was to keep a lookout for SS patrols, so that these eleven Poles in civilian clothes – another privilege – could hide the entrance to the tunnel they were digging. Their clothes made this adventure possible.

Just a chance of success. They were willing to take it.

So I was the innocent witness of their escape attempt.

The tunnel went from the building they were putting up out into the little wood beyond the lookout towers, manned day and night by SS guards.

Eleven men who decided, one summer evening, that that was the night to crawl to freedom. The dream was in their grasp. Yes, tonight's the night.
Tonight's the night. That's what they've decided.

It only took one prisoner, just one, to betray them to the SS and end the dream. What was his price?
A loaf of bread? Two, three, four...?
Who knows. The price of survival.

Eleven men who hadn't thought it would just take one starving prisoner to chance by and seal their fate.

Eleven men who hung from ropes swaying in the wind.

In massed ranks, we all had to watch.
Drop your head, and a gun butt thumped it back up.
Was it ourselves that we were inwardly contemplating, as we watched those bodies gradually stop squirming and stiffen?
For hours we were forced to witness the last convulsions of eleven men's desire to live.

Eleven of them there were, who would rather risk being hanged for the chance of a life of freedom than endure the slow death programmed for them by the Nazis.

Eleven Polish builders, ten plus their kapo, from Katowice, down the road.

All our eyes raised to watch, forced by gun butts to watch those bodies. In the satellite camp of Auschwitz, the camp where death was guaranteed.

I think I must have been the only one to mourn that 'good' kapo – socialist, resister, and antisemite.

Auschwitz — music to make, from the blood of hell

Auschwitz, l'en faire un chant

In the summer of 1944, over half a century ago, two of my fellow-sufferers and fellow-slaves in the camp at Jaworzno were murdered in two different, but typical, ways. Two men who were dear to me.

One was Henri, a Belgian Jew and resister who had been fighting for an ideal of democracy since leading anti-fascist troops in the Spanish civil war.
Unfortunately, democracy can no longer be defended with pitchforks and flails, the implements of peace – confronted with the deadliest weapons of the age, we have to use machine guns and artillery.

Anyway, at the end of an exhausting day – every day the same in the camp – Henri wearily turned to me and said: 'I've had enough.'
I asked:
'Was your day worse than usual?'
'No, I'm just worn out. I can't move, I can't even think.'

And we both lay down, on the same palliasse, to get our usual night-mare-ridden sleep. In the morning, I woke up next to a cold, rigid corpse. In once dropping his guard, he had lost all power of resistance.

The rule today, as it was yesterday, is never to drop your guard; always keep your fists up, if you want to give your children and their children a life of peace and love.

❧

The other was a docker from Salonika whom we called Greco. He was in the same labour squad as Henri and me, and he used to hum to himself as he worked, the same tune over and over (I can still hear how it started); it was a habit he had got into years before, carrying heavy loads round the docks.
But Jaworzno isn't Salonika, and SS guards aren't the gaffers of peace-time.

I was an old hand, seasoned by dozens of kickings and beatings. I understood our tormentors' mentality, and I kept telling him: 'They might at a pinch be prepared to let you scream in pain and fear as they beat you and torture you, or cry yourself to death for your lost life. But for you to hum, here, wounds their pride; it's an insult to their system and their determination to destroy you.'

And, one blazing day in August 1944, they duly kicked and beat him to death, with his own shovel.

These memories have come back up from the depths of the oblivion I had buried them in, with so many others.

AUSCHWITZ — BORROWED TIME, COMMITTED BLOOD

AUSCHWITZ, L'ENGAGEMENT

In this place of solitude and beauty,
Château-sous-Bois,
The fiftieth anniversary of freedom.
Fifty years of life
I have snatched back from death.

THE COMMITMENT

Horror and atrocity
Today and tomorrow should be pierced through
In unending combat
By the luminous dignity of every human being.

To want
Intensely to live,
To want passionately to love
For dread of growing old.
To want
Painfully, infinitely to embrace
Life
For dread of deadly nothingness.
Eluding discouragement
Through anger and indignation,
I use the past
To construct the present
And preserve the future
For coming generations.

Toi – You,

It really is you, that beggar?

The beggar of Jaworzno.

Branded with shame for ever,

And humiliation for good measure.

Never, ever again to have to beg, for anything.

To ask for anything.

PART TWO

Anthology
and selected paintings

Dark days
Luminous days
My love is in the present

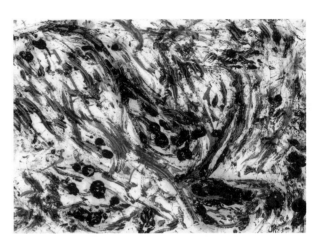

Forced at last to quit their violin,
My crooked fingers
Took pen and brush instead
To write my ideas down,
To set my music to colour,
On X-ray plates and paper,
To help me battle
To transcend dignity.

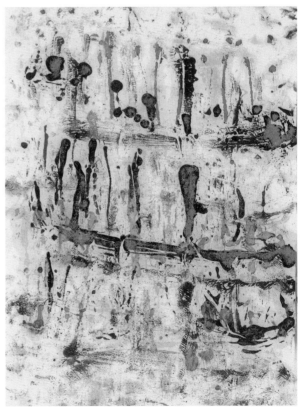

Tell it and tell it again, and again

The camp, the fantasies.
The anger, the tears.
The tenacity.
The violin.
The sheer chance.

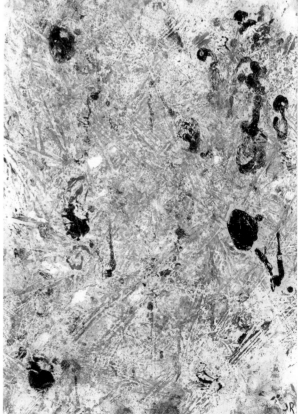

Taking off your clothes seems natural
at home.
Very different, with a hundred of you together
for the first time.
The others all just so many mirrors.
Is there anything quite like that first evening
in a concentration camp?
Head shaved.
Disinfected.
The showers?

They built pyramids
With the help of a million victims,
With the help of a million men.
And we
Have helped to kill,
To annihilate, whole millions of men.

Which leaves
Those who needed no help:
The starved, the tortured.

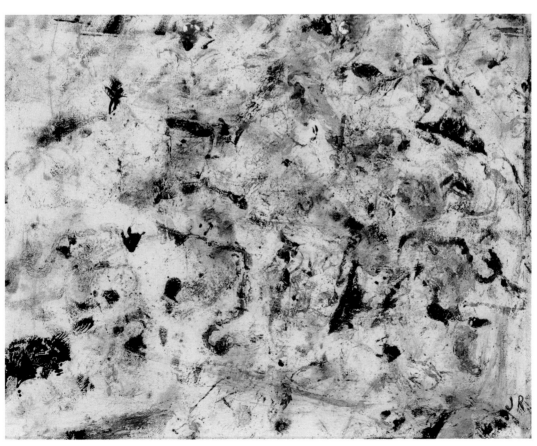

Had enough,
Can't go on,
Needing help,
Last resort,
Offered help,
Doesn't help.

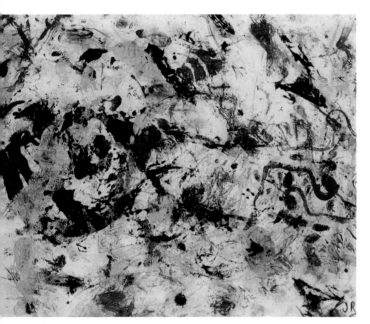

My cries,
Amidst the most utter indifference.
Against mendacity, manipulation, hatred.
Any hatred.

Yesterday. Today.
He did what he could.
They did nothing when they could.
What worries me is not the guilt
of individuals
But their so-called innocence.

The need to inform, the things to ask oneself.
With that ever heavier weight to lift,
The duty to live and bear witness.

A journey through horror – well, so what.
Shut in, locked up.
A human cabbage, having no dreams,
No utopia, no ideal.

Some reckoned: better off dead.

Starving... Starving... Starved.
Dead.

Became what I'd never have dreamt I'd be.

The earth turns all right.
My head's turned out wrong
On this earth.
My head's not right.
I'm going round all right,
In circles.

I can't manage to talk abstraction today,
Or butterflies or little flowers.
I'm getting my message pictures from those
Who vanished as smoke,
To beautiful, cruel nature's
Total indifference,
Becoming what *they'd* never have dreamt
they'd be...

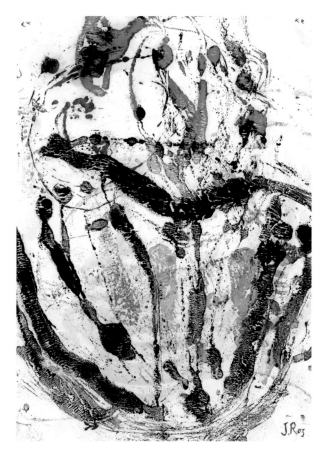

How many-times-torn is life, my life,
The rope round the throat so tight I tug and reknot
The knots as best I can.
I've lived a switchback life,
The fairground ride you face alone
As the crowd looks on.
Life's a merry-go-round, up and down,
Perpetual motion:
Tragedies or joys.

Is this not reason enough to despair?
To Sainte-Ode for treatment, to Switzerland,
Romania, Budapest.
Count up all the clinics, all the medication.
So many setbacks
Sap what courage I have left.

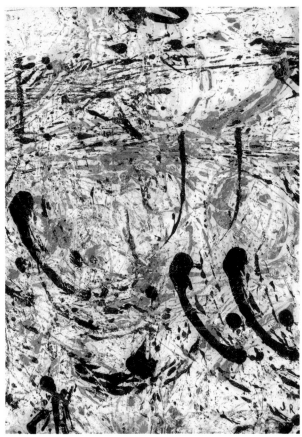

Might we be so very self-centred
We're blind,
Deaf,
Or in another world?
A lot of people are so small
They can neither live nor think but earthbound.
Some are so very small
They never see anything
But under the counter.

Tell only of mini-shock-horrors that today's
mini-individuals can cope with.

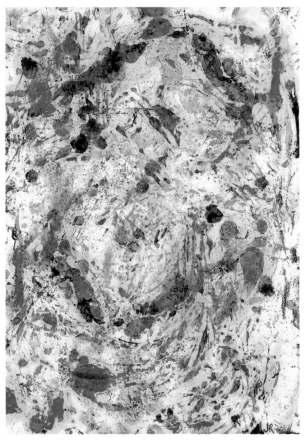

I have a lot of unpublishable texts,
too desperate or too disjointed
for any reader.

Here, at Jaworzno,
Is where birds glad to be alive,
And not to be
Beings
Like the beings here
Captive, shut in,
Are glad and free to sing.

Fying since whenever.
Soaring, off the ground.
– Oh yes, many times he's done it.
Flying, effortlessly up
To the stars.
But is he any more human?

Wait for the springtime.
Make it to springtime.
Meantime
Gain time.

Seize the time,
Seize again
Those numbered days.
Make them, happily, time gained.

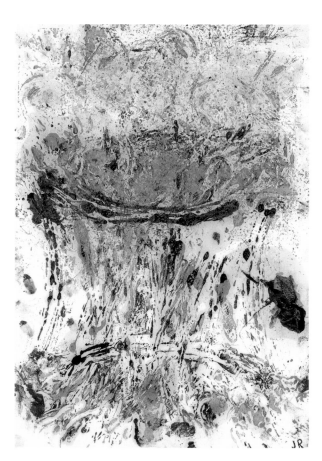

How,
In all conscience, after that camp,
Was I able to bear the burden and not
destroy myself,
To stop
Having to think,
Having to speak.

Happily, music is not denied me.

Scores of talks; 'Make it short' – so short
they last.
Not just lessons on the victims of our past,
But seeking to prevent the most evil
Of evils
Returning now or in the future.

Afraid of going wrong, I make notes to help.
But what would I do without my music?
The notes sing inside me,
No matter if my ears are growing deaf.

Had I but been able
To lock my tears into words, sounds, colours,
Not to drown them,
But to give them body.

137

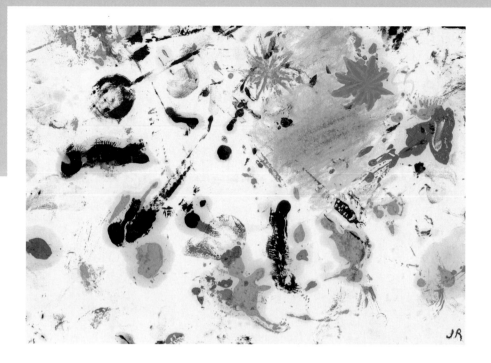

To each his each.
To each his dream.
To each according to his reality.
To each according to his mistakes.

Here I am alone again,
The solitude hospital always aggravates,
Steeped in anxiety and fear.
Certainties back in doubt.

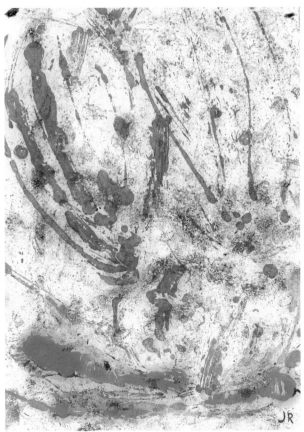

I've given up wondering what infirmity
to settle for.
My hopelessness I've hidden
Behind hope,
Like something to cling to after shipwreck.
Every encounter's a crossroads of possibili-
ties.
Take what suits and suffer what doesn't
From these crosssroads,
Paths met,
Crossed,
All of them
Leading
To headstones.

What an illusion, that no lifetime's worth
more than another,
When equality only rules
In the cemetery.
Dying also needs,
Even after fifty years' surviving,
Someone with you,
A caress,
A farewell.

How many among us
Have been able to arrange themselves a life?
Forgotten to prepare themselves a death?
For my part, striving
To ignore the fated, logical conclusion,
Might I also have forgotten
To prepare mine?
Though for some years now
Condemned to converse only
With the walls in my flat,
I go on trying to understand
– Me, the sceptic born and sworn –
Executioners and victims: all so blind.

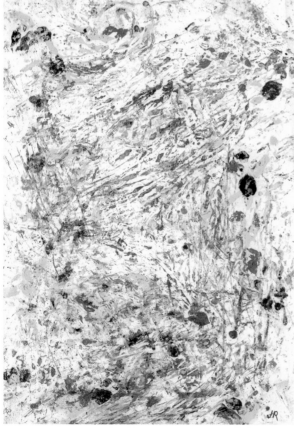

Tell it
And tell it again, and again.
The just, the unjust,
The what,
The what, the how, the why.
All is handed down.

Might I have left no mark, no adequate trace?

Auschwitz – Blood gone with the hot air
Auschwitz – Burnt blood, incense still in the
wind
Auschwitz – Music to make, from the blood of
hell
Auschwitz – Borrowed time, committed blood.

Now
It's your turn.
Do it, don't do it –
It's your choice,
Without me for once.

Today, in 1998.
Why not, in 1999,
Still ask yourself the questions?

Face with blue eyes.

There appears a face.
Whose? Anyone's.
Just a face.
Mirror to the loneliness of one
Who can no longer embrace,
Or get his breath squeezed out in a bear-hug;
And yet wants to live, to keep on going.

Memory.
Digging down into deepest self
With tools rusty
From fifty or sixty years' living, surviving.

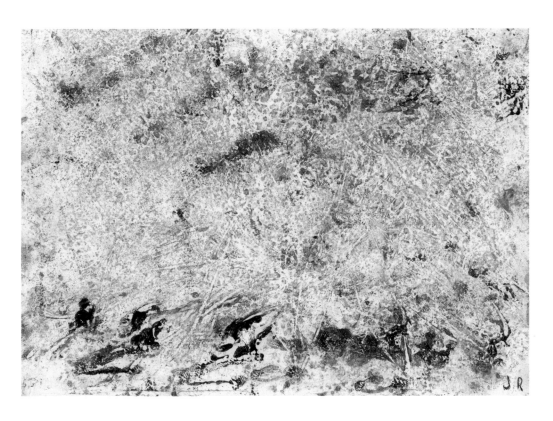

How?
How to live afterwards,
An end deliberately premature.

How to escape.
To live to live
Self-absorbed, or for money, or creation,
Love or affection.
To live one more time,
To live for a day, a month,
A year, eternity.

To live lovingly, warmly.

Don't refuse,
Don't destroy yourself.

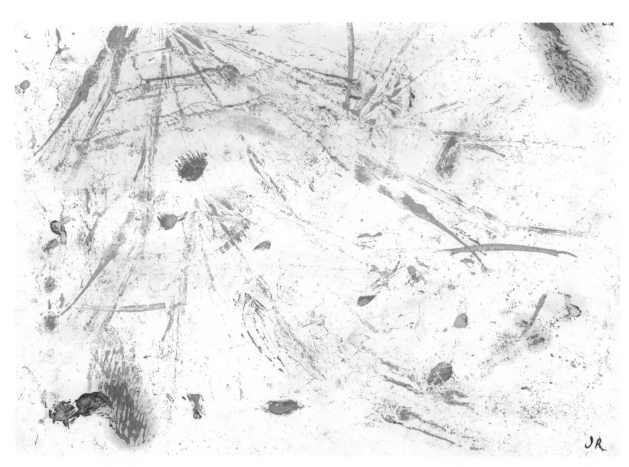

Let the image of a friend be a beautiful tree,
A house be a place where all are free to be,
Where the rule is love and respect for another,
That other chosen from among so many others.

Any love or joy or happiness
Passing within heart's reach
Is for seizing –
Unhesitatingly, unquestioningly.
Even if tomorrow's not the dreamt-of
dawn,
Even if time passing strikes
a chord of disquiet,
Even sometimes echoing old sorrows,
That wealth of things you garner
will be a gift.

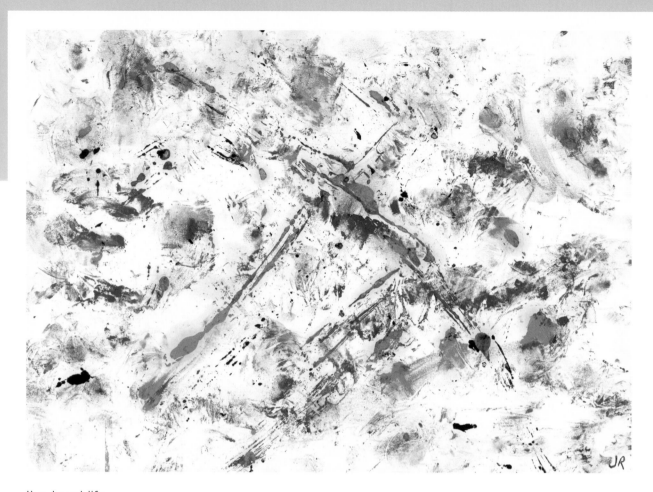

I've loved life,
My life,
The whole of it.

I've loved life,
My life,
Even the suffering
I've sometimes wished for release from.

Turn love into a rocket
Sent to all the moons
That are our dreams.

Flow the sweet honey,
Soother of bitterness and the soul,
Coater, caresser, licker-round
Inside
And out.

Love,
Which so far
Has never left me,
Me, the Resister.

'My first drawing', inspired by Henry Moore

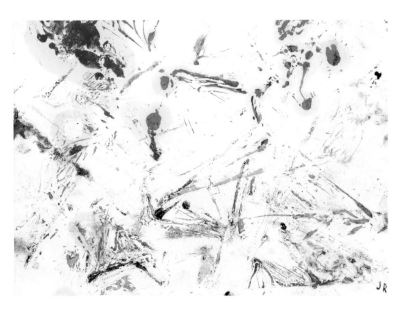

There are
The blues and the reds,
The yellows and browns,
The blacks and the whites,
The oranges and greens
To create, starting today,
A more humane world.

My love isn't Eve's, or Adam's,
From the dawn of time.
My love is in the present.

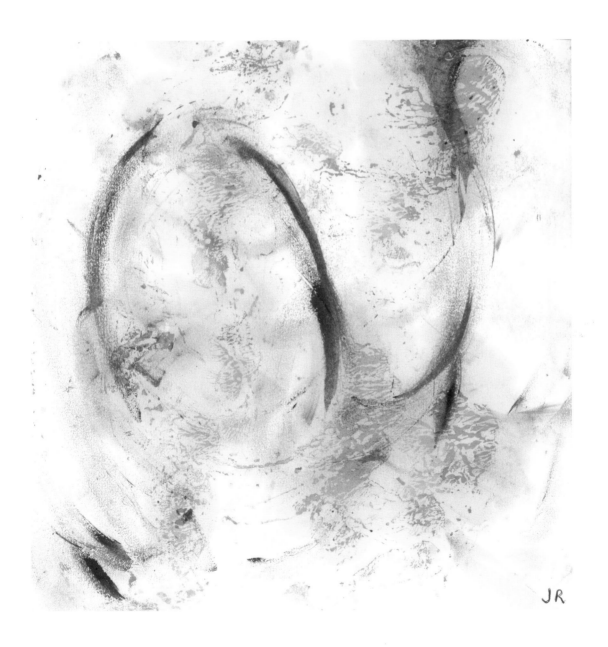

JR

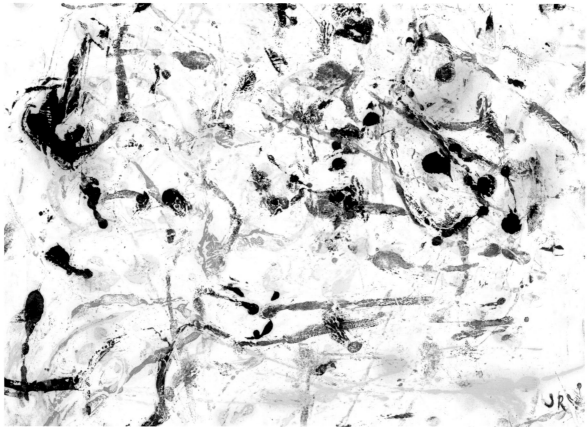

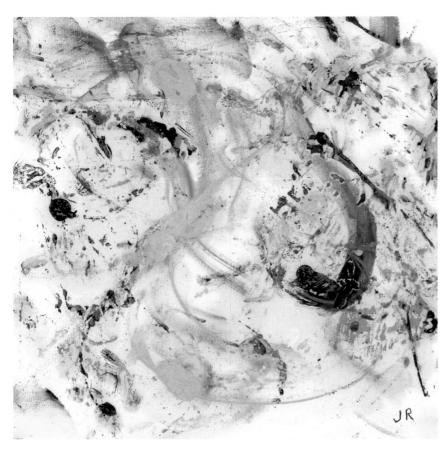

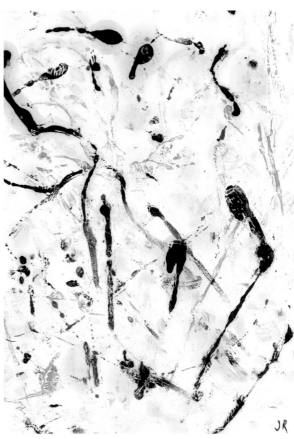

Leaving a note.
My note.

Seeing is not knowing;
Knowing is not thinking;
Thinking is not acting.

Dirtying my hands with painting,
Not to have to dirty them in life.
Doing all to make beauty and good
For life,
The one true good we possess.

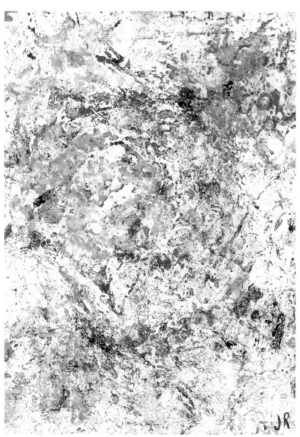

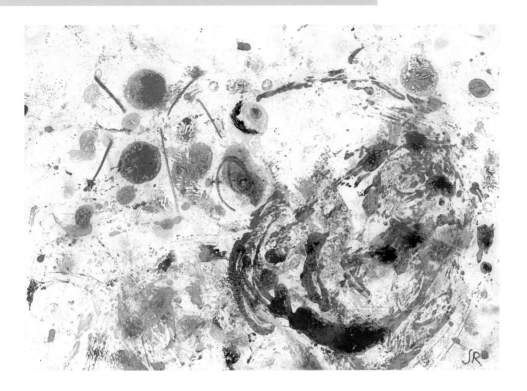

Pessimism of mind and reason.

Optimism of will and commitment.

I have abused my humour

To humour my moods.

Nothing comes from nothing, everything from everything.

My gloomy head is ringing,
Eyes in dislocated orbit
round the brain,
But my heart is singing –
I'm coming home again.

Let them call on me to help
And question me too,
Those who tell me
Of the haps and mishaps of this world,
For me to feel I'm useful too.

Biography

It is to you, Jacques,
and to people like you,
who have made the struggle against
fascism and injustice their first priority,
that we owe our freedom.

Andrée.

Jacques Rozenberg
1922–1999

BORN GRODZIK, POLAND, 1922.
MOVED TO BELGIUM WITH HIS PARENTS
SHORTLY AFTERWARDS.
DIED BRUSSELS, 1 AUGUST 1999

Studied the violin, alongside attendance at secondary school. The war put an end to these studies, but the love of music informed his whole life.

Working for an underground Resistance publisher, he was arrested and taken to Dosselin barracks in Mechlin in April 1943.
Being Jewish, he was deported to Auschwitz on 31 July of that year, on transport XXI. In mid-January 1945, with Soviet troops approaching, the camp was evacuated by the retreating Germans. For the next two months, the Death March took him via a number of other camps to Dachau, where he was liberated by the Americans.

A musicologist, he was best known as Director of the Brussels region Record Library (subsequently the Media Library).

He was a mixture of realism, irony, scepticism and idealism. His was the pessimism of the mind and the optimism of commitment. In spite of – or perhaps because of – illness, he took up writing, and then painting. His pictures were small, because, not having a studio, he had no space to paint on a larger scale. He used pencil, brush and, occasionally, his fingers.
He converted his perception of music into visual perception, giving it abstract, non-figurative form, and transposing onto paper events, both tragic and joyous, that he had experienced.
This material gradually began to attract praise for its subtlety of pigment and intensity of colour.

For the harsh palette and the impact of those colours were the hall-marks of Jacques Rozenberg's painterly idiom. As he used to say: 'I'm not really interested in lines and angles, more in sensual curves, like my beloved violin, or the archetypal woman.'

In December 1997, he took part in a colloquium organised by the Auschwitz Foundation at the Francophone Community of Belgium building, on the theme of 'The memory of Auschwitz in contemporary art', illustrating his contribution with six of his paintings.

This was the first of a number of joint or one-man exhibitions.

'My music in colour'
Hôtel communal, Etterbeek (Brussels)
4 May – 8 June 2000

Paintings on X-ray plates
UPJB – Parcours d'artistes. Commune de Saint-Gilles (Brussels)
May 2000

'Jacques Rozenberg, on freedom and tolerance'
VUB. Free University of Brussels
15 November – 15 December 2000

'Painting and writing after Auschwitz'
Stedelijke Openbare Bibliotheek Aarschot
19–27 January 2001

'Painting and writing after Auschwitz'
Centre Culturel de Tubize
23 March – 1 April 2001

'I have met hatred'
Centre Culturel de Braine-le-Comte – Salle Baudouin IV
11–23 November 2001

'Painting and writing after Auschwitz'
Maison de la Culture de Tournai
1–24 March 2002

'Homage to Jacques Rozenberg'
A whole room is hung with his paintings
UPJB – Parcours d'artistes. Commune de Saint-Gilles (Brussels)
May 2002

'Freedom and tolerance'
Campaign against fascism and racism
FGTB Brussels
20 February – 26 March 2003

'Don Quixote'
UPJB – Parcours d'artistes. Commune de Saint-Gilles (Brussels)
May 2004

Exhibition and presentation of the book
'Hommage' in the Dutch version
A.B.V.V. – Leuven
November 2005

Exhibition Painting and Writing after Auschwitz
European School – Brussels
February–March 2006

Congress A.B.V.V. – Blankenberghe
8 May 2006

Lecture with the participation of Monique Dorsel, Agnès Ben Simon,
Claire Pahaut and Andrée Caillet
10 May 2006
Exhibition 10–18 May 2006
Théatre Poème – Brussels

Various paintings
U.P.J.B. – Parcours d'artistes
Commune de Saint-Gilles (Brussels)
May 2006

Lecture with the participation of Claire Pahaut and Andrée Caillet
17 November 2006
Exhibition 17 November – 2 December 2006
Royal Military Academy – Brussels

Reading by Ian Higgins
Various paintings
'The Little Gallery' – Pittenweem, Scotland
May 2007

Fleurs de Tendresse
U.P.J.B. – Parcours d'artistes, 20th anniversary
Commune de Saint-Gilles (Brussels)
May 2008

Forthcoming exhibitions in Belgium and abroad

'The Tree of Liberty'

I OWE WARMEST THANKS TO:

The friends who encouraged me in putting together this book, which –
while he in no way thought of it as a tribute – was so close to Jacques'
heart.

Claire Pahaut, co-chair, 'Démocratie ou barbarie' (Democracy or
Barbarism), for her efficiency and help, her judicious advice, her patience
and her friendship.

Virginie Denaeyer, graphic designer, to whose sensitive and intelligent
reading of the text and images this book owes its powerful visual
impact.

Claude-Thérèse Pirson, founder-president of the Service Club Soroptimist
International Brussels-Sablon, and Dr Guy Themelin, trustee of the
Fondation Rozenberg-Caillet 'Mains ouvertes – Dignité de vie', both of
whom answered my questions with sagacity and affection.

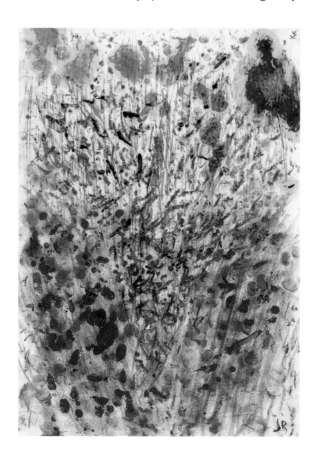

'Wait, don't rush,
there may still be something for you to do,
a job to see through, nothing heroic,
just enough to justify your journey.'

Printed in Ghent, June 2008